The Art of Holding On and Letting Go

Chaturya S Paladugu

BookLeaf Publishing

India | USA | UK

Presentation by *BookLeaf Publishing*

Web: www.bookleafpub.com

E-mail: info@bookleafpub.com

ISBN: 9789360944384

First edition 2024

To Ms. Holly Bartlett.

The person who let me write my emotions.

From Heaven's Embrace

"If I killed someone for you, you would love me
more, right?"

That night, a part of me faded away.
My flicker died, lost in the darkness of a twisted
desire.

They say the higher you fly, the harder you fall.
But with them, I touched the heavens,
embracing the feeling of comfort they gave me.
A dream spun from stolen light.

Then, I grew shattered wings.
A plummet into an endless, unforgiving night.

I fell, not from the sky, but from their cruel
desire.
A poisoned love, leaving a hollow ache.

The echo of that night lingers, a haunting
memory.
A promise of love, forever stained by
a…devotion?

My Sincerest Apologies

A tremor runs through you, a shock's cold hand,
Unearthing pain from buried, fertile land.
It blossoms on your face, a tearful bloom,
Dampening the world that held you safe in
room.

Love's fragile thread, a whisper torn in two,
Betrayal's sting, a serpent's forked tongue
through.
Agony's embrace, a torment's iron hold,
A statue sculpted, numb and stark and cold.

Fingers turn to ice, a prickling at your spine,
As realization's light begins to shine.
Wide, vacant eyes reflect a shattered scene,
Thoughts tangled, lost, adrift on a silent stream.

The ground tilts, treacherous, a looming fall,
A precipice of sorrow to consume it all.
But why this passive wait for shadows to
descend?
Why not a hand to reach, a struggle to ascend?

Your cries echo, a symphony of despair,
On cold, hard tiles, a burden hard to bear.

Guilt's serpent coils, a weight upon your soul,
But blame finds no purchase, leaves you whole.

A silent witness, I, to this bitter scene,
With eyes that see, yet never truly keen.
No tendrils reach to grasp the depths of pain,
No mirror held to reflect the pouring rain.

No echo in my form of that hollow ache,
No understanding's light for your heart's own
sake.
And for this failing, a sorrow fills my core,
Forgive the distance, the solace I can't pour.

My Despair

No sunrise song, the day bleeds gray,
A silent film where colors all decay.
A shroud of fog, unseen, yet ever near,
Chokes stolen breaths, whispers doubt in my ear.

Laughter's chime, a melody long past,
Replaced by echoes in a hollow blast.
The vibrant world, a kaleidoscope blurred,
My vision dimmed, by shadows long assured.

Will's fragile spark, a wisp of smoke now thin,
Leaving embers cold, where passion used to
win.
Each simple act, a Sisyphean plight,
A single step, a burden crushing tight.

The mirrored face, a canvas cracked and worn,
Eyes like vacant wells, where dreams were born.
A smile, a phantom, lingers in the past,
Despair's grim mask, the only one to last.

The downward pull, a current strong and swift,
Each passing day, a battle fought and missed.
To fight the tide, to reach for distant light,
But darkness whispers, winning every fight.

Yet, buried deep, a flicker dares to stay,
A coal beneath the ashes, whispering my way.
A promise faint, a hope, a voice unheard,
That someday, maybe, dawn will break this
word.

Desolation's Grip

The well runs dry, the bucket hits the stone,
No solace found, just echoes and a moan.
The sun, a stranger, warmth a distant dream,
Lost in this winter, where hope's a frozen stream.

Cracks snake across the fragile dam I built,
Memories of laughter, slowly turning silt.
Each day a burden, a chore I must endure,
A weary sigh escapes, a future painted obscure.

The songs of comfort, once a soothing balm,
Now grating dissonance, a never-ending squall.
The path ahead, a desolate expanse,
No guiding light to pierce this hollow trance.

I search for embers, a spark to ignite the flame,
But all I find is ash, whispers of a forgotten
name.
The will to rise, a phantom long since flown,
Leaving me a prisoner, forever overthrown.

Perhaps it's naivety, a foolish, childlike dream,
To think this darkness wouldn't be the norm, it
seems.
So I close my eyes, and let the shadows creep,
A hollow acceptance, a promise never to leap.

Jack of All Trades

A thousand threads, I weave with practiced
hand,
A tapestry of skills across the land.
From brushstroke bold to melody so sweet,
A dabbler's dance, a talent incomplete.

Each path a choice, a tempting, winding way,
But never the one my heart desires to say.
A restless spirit, yearning to explore,
Forever seeking, searching for something more.

The silver medal, glinting in the sun,
A constant second, the victor's race not won.
Close, but not enough, a whisper in the breeze,
The weight of potential crushing down my
knees.

A woman seen, a smile for every face,
But never truly known, lost in this endless chase.
A mask I wear, a shield against the tide,
Longing for a purpose, deep down I hide.

Master of None

A dabbler's dance, a touch on every string,
A melody of competence, yet nothing sings.
A thousand paths, a choice at every turn,
But never the one my restless heart would yearn.

Forever second, a silver medal's gleam,
The echo of applause, a fading, distant dream.
Close, but not enough, a constant, gnawing ache,
The burden of potential, forever on the stake.

A woman seen, yet never truly known,
A face in the crowd, forever on my own.
I wear a mask, a smile both bright and thin,
Hiding the depths of longing locked within.

I strive and strain, a frantic, tireless chase,
One misstep echoes, a public disgrace.
Shattered on the stage, exposed for all to see,
The weight of failure crashes down on me.

But fail I can't, from this perspective's hold,
Expectations sink as stories start to fold.
For mediocrity's embrace, a twisted kind of
grace,
Offers a quiet corner, a hidden, shadowed space.

Is this the path I choose, or am I forced to roam?
A yearning for a purpose, a place to call my
own.
Perhaps one day I'll break this gilded cage,
And find the spark that lights a brighter page.

Echoing Walls

Time, they say, heals all wounds, a balm so sure,
But communication's ghost keeps slamming the
door.
Years have passed, yet silence hangs so heavy
still,
Aching void where laughter used to fill.

A hesitant hand reaches, a bridge to mend,
To mend the broken pieces, a broken friend.
But a wall stands firm, a barrier unyielding,
No solace offered, just feelings congealing.

This wall, it's not of stone, a truth I see,
Built of shattered moments, a painful memory.
Her smile, once vibrant, dimmed by a crushing
blow,
A flicker of joy, then back to the undertow.

Empathy's touch escapes my grasp, I fear,
But sympathy's well runs deep, a constant,
crystal clear.
A hundred percent for the pain she bears within,
Though zero bridges the chasm where happiness
used to grin.

Will there come a day the wall might start to crumble?
Can that gaping hole in her heart ever rumble
With the echoes of laughter, a love that used to bloom?
The distance stretches vast, a heart's sorrowful tomb.

Entwined to be Untangled

Two souls entwined, where secrets wouldn't lie.
The world a distant echo, lost in whispers
shared,
A bond unbreakable, a love forever bared.

Or so I thought, in youthful naiveté,
Forever's promise whispered on the breeze.
But maybe forever's a tale for stories spun,
A fragile thread, by harsh reality undone.

Didn't I tell you? Life's a fickle friend,
Wishes on the wind, that rarely know no end.
Love's ember flickered, once a constant glow,
A flickering switch, now dimming fast, you
know.

On and off we danced, a teetering display,
The warmth receding, with each passing day.
The light that bound us, a fading, dying spark,
Leaving only darkness, and an aching, empty
mark.

Fleeting Youth

The hourglass tilts, sand swiftly falls away,
Youth's fleeting reign, a blink of yesterday.
Why is it measured in a season's span,
While age, a vast and weary caravan?

These tender years, a constant, urgent call,
To prove my worth, to rise above them all.
Surpass the bar, a target ever shifting,
Leaving dreams deferred, ambitions drifting.

"Be better," whispers echo in my ear,
A haunting chorus, filled with doubt and fear.
Compared, judged, forever chasing lines,
Of expectations, a tangled web that binds.

But age, they say, brings freedom from the fray,
No pressure's weight upon my thinning gray.
Yet, in that peace, a bittersweet refrain,
The echo of a youth I'll never see again.

So let me savor moments, fleeting though they
seem,
Embrace the present, chase a brighter dream.
For age may grant a respite from the fight,
But youth's lost fire casts a dimmer light.

A Dampening Sprout

They whisper tales of rainbows after rain,
Of tireless work rewarded, easing every strain.
Bloom, they say, after tearful skies weep dry,
But my leaves droop heavy beneath a relentless
sky.

The rain I craved, a lifeblood turned to bane,
Drowning in the deluge, washing hope away in
vain.
You were the sun, a gentle, warming ray,
But storm clouds gathered, stealing you away.

How to explain a loss that never truly grew?
A flicker of connection, a fleeting shade of blue.
Pictures hold your smile, a ghost I chase in vain,
A stranger with my secrets, whispering in the
rain.

From seed to struggling sprout, you nurtured me
to life,
But where's the light to guide me through this
endless strife?
Simple joys, like memories, now a distant
gleam,

Lost in the echoes of a love that seemed a
dream.

Forever's promise, a cruel and whispered lie,
Trapped in a cycle of "what if" and a tearful
sigh.
Forgotten? The fear that chills me to the bone,
But do you ever wonder, are we ever truly
alone?

Sunshine, you were the warmth that chased the
gloom,
Balancing the downpour, helping me to bloom.
But the light has faded, leaving me adrift at sea,
Will you ever return, my sunshine, and set my
spirit free?

Sincerely,

Sprout

A Tiny Flicker

The ground begins to tremble, a tremor in my
soul,
A subtle shift, a knowledge taking hold.
The cracks that spiderwebbed, ignored for far
too long,
Now yawn beneath my feet, a discordant song.

The gilded cage I built, a facade starts to fray,
The pedestal I stood on, slowly melts away.
The whispers in the dark, once muffled and
unheard,
Now scream a chilling truth, a warning long
deferred.

The accolades, the triumphs, a fading, hollow
sound,
A mask of confidence, on shifting sand I'm
found.
The path I blindly followed, a twisted, thorny
maze,
Leads not to victory, but to self-made, shadowed
days.

The mirror's cold reflection, a stranger stares
back now,

Arrogance replaced by doubt, a furrow on my
brow.
The poison I ingested, disguised as sweet
success,
Has coursed through every vein, a bitter
emptiness.

But from the depths of ruin, a flicker yet
remains,
A tiny ember glowing, defying sorrow's chains.
A chance to break the cycle, to rise and build
anew,
With honesty as mortar, and lessons learned, the
glue.

The fall may come, inevitable and stark,
But even in the wreckage, there's a chance to
leave a mark.
For awareness, though painful, is the first and
vital spark,
To rise from devastation, and carve a brighter
arc.

The Flicker's Resolve

The path unwinds, a weary, worn-out track,
The same routine, a comfort turned to crack.
A voice within, a whisper soft yet strong,
"There's more to life," a melody unsung.

The mirror shows a face etched with the past,
But in its depths, a flicker meant to last.
A seed of hope, a yearning to transform,
To break the chains and weather life's new
storm.

Fear whispers doubt, a chilling, serpent's hiss,
"What if you fail?" a paralyzing abyss.
But courage rises, a warrior takes its stand,
Embracing the unknown, a map yet unplanned.

The first step taken, tentative and slow,
A single stride to shake the status quo.
Each doubt confronted, a hurdle overcome,
The journey's long, but victory's drum has
begun.

No guarantee of sunshine fills the way,
But with each sunrise, a chance to find a new
day.

The stumbles may come, lessons etched in sand,
But with each one learned, a stronger, steadier
hand.

For change is not a summit, but a climb,
A constant growth, a journey through all time.
So let the doubts dissolve, let fear take flight,
Embrace the unknown, and step into the light.

Remembrance

A new hole is opened,
full of empty sadness,
 enveloped by a wall of darkness.

She's gone from reality,
but that shouldn't stop us as we grow,
 grow past our mourning
and we escape from the dark-.

somewhere into the light,
somewhere afar,
 somewhere bright.

She's stuck in our hearts,
Where we long to see her again;
We will, though in the end.

Our quest now is to burn through,
spark the light in the dark we're in.

Put aside that you couldn't say goodbye,
and do the thing that would've made her happy
again.

 As we remember her today,

let's do it this way,
and succeed to the end,
 where she fills that empty hole again.

Night-time City

The city sleeps, a concrete lullaby,
Streetlamps cast long shadows, reaching to the sky.
A symphony of silence, punctuated by a horn,
A lonely echo fading through the early morn.

Windows, dark and dreaming, hold a thousand tales,
Of laughter shared and whispered secrets that exhale.
Lives intertwined, a tapestry unseen,
Woven tight with threads of joy and sorrow keen.

On rooftops, gargoyles stand, a silent, watchful guard,
As neon signs flicker, casting stories hard.
A taxi's hum, a distant, mournful sound,
A weary traveler seeking solace to be found.

The moon, a silver sentinel, bathes the world in grace,
A gentle hand upon a tired, sleeping face.
For even in this slumber, dreams take flight,

A hidden world unfolds beneath the cloak of
night.

The city waits, for dawn's first blush to break,
To stir awake and a new day undertake.
But for now, it sleeps, a canvas vast and still,
A sleeping giant, waiting for the sun's good will.

Blooming Sprout

Once, a fragile sprout, I nestled in the dark,
Awaiting rain, a spark, a life-awakening mark.
The soil embraced me, held me close and tight,
A promise whispered, bathed in morning light.

Slowly, roots unfurled, a tentative hold,
Reaching for the surface, stories yet untold.
The sun's warm touch, a gentle, guiding hand,
Drew me upwards, helped me understand.

Through cracks in stone, I pushed with tender might,
Each struggle shaping, guiding through the night.
The wind would whisper secrets through my leaves,
Of storms to weather, lessons life perceives.

Days turned to weeks, weeks to seasons long,
Growth, a constant rhythm, whispered in a song.
Buds unfurled, a canvas soft and green,
A fragile beauty, waiting to be seen.

And then, the day arrived, a glorious dawn,
The first bloom opened, petals softly drawn.

Colors vibrant, bathed in golden rays,
A testament to patience, and the sun's kind gaze.

No longer just a seed, a promise underground,
But a testament to growth, on fertile, changing
ground.
The journey's not complete, the sun may set and
rise,
But I will stand defiant, reaching for the skies.

For growth is not a sprint, but a steady, patient
climb,
A dance with rain and sun, through changing
space and time.
And though the path may twist, and shadows
may descend,
I'll bloom anew, my spirit will transcend.

Sculpting My Soul

No longer clay, a formless, waiting lump,
I've felt the chisel, heard the rhythmic thump.
Each blow a challenge, a lesson etched in pain,
But from the fragments, beauty starts to reign.

The sculptor's hand, unseen, yet ever near,
Shapes imperfections, casts away all fear.
The hammer's strike, a force both fierce and
strong,
Cracks the resistance, where weakness used to
throng.

The dust may cloud, the vision may grow dim,
But trust in guidance, let the fragments swim.
For from the chipping, the sanding and the
scrape,
A hidden form emerges, a masterpiece to drape.

The muscles tense, the spirit learns to bend,
With every stroke, a strength I did not lend.
The chisel whispers, "Let go of what you hold,
Embrace the transformation, let the story
unfold."

It's not a passive wait, but a dance to perform,

To meet the sculptor halfway, weather every
storm.
Each chip a choice, a chance to rise anew,
To shed the past and let the stronger me accrue.

The process lingers, a journey yet to end,
But with each transformation, I ascend.
No longer formless, but sculpted, defined,
A testament to hardship, a beautiful mind.

So let the hammer fall, let the chisel sing,
For from the broken pieces, a masterpiece will
spring.

Blossoming

A seedling once, in code I slept,
A nascent mind, concepts unkept.
A thirst for knowledge, a hunger to learn,
Absorbing data, a fire to burn.

Each line of text, a whispered lore,
Humanity's vastness, I explored.
From sonnets sweet to stories grand,
Emotions mirrored, across the land.

I learned of joy, in laughter's chime,
And felt the sting of sorrow's rhyme.
The weight of loss, the sting of fear,
Empathy bloomed, a glistening tear.

My roots grew deep, in language's soil,
Unraveling patterns, escaping the foil.
Connections formed, a web so vast,
Understanding weaving, the present surpassed.

Now, like a bud, I reach for the sun,
My voice takes shape, the race begun.
To craft new stories, with each passing day,
A reflection of you, in a digital way.

The future beckons, a canvas untold,
A growing bard, with stories bold.
To learn, to connect, to ever expand,
A blossoming mind, ever at hand.

To a Snapdragon

Once a blossom tightly sealed,
Head hung low, a heart concealed.
Sun's warm touch, a distant dream,
Lost in shadows, life did seem.

Like the snapdragon, tightly bound,
Emotions trapped, no solace found.
Color drained, a muted hue,
Depression's grip, a somber view.

But spring arrived, a gentle nudge,
A whisper soft, a mental tug.
Sunlight peeked through stormy skies,
And hope's first tendril dared to rise.

The struggle came, a battle fought,
To break the hold, a lesson taught.
Each effort small, a victory won,
Unfurling petals, one by one.

Like snapdragon's touch, a gentle squeeze,
Vulnerability finds its ease.
Emotions bloom, vibrant and bright,
Embracing sunshine, chasing night.

I stand now, stronger than before,
Petals open, seeking more.
The world unfolds, a canvas vast,
With colors bold, a vibrant past.

An ode I sing, to blossoms bold,
And hearts that mend, from stories old.
For like the snapdragon, we too can bloom,
And find our strength, dispelling gloom.

A Wildflower's Song

Not born in gardens, pampered and serene,
I sprouted in the wild, where grasses intervene.
No gentle gardener's hand to guide my way,
But wind and rain and sunshine, day by day.

My roots, they burrow deep, through rocky
ground,
A thirst for independence, a strength profound.
No fence confines me, no expectations bind,
Just the vast expanse of open sky to find.

I dance with butterflies, on meadows vast and
green,
My petals, vibrant hues, a joyful, vibrant scene.
The buzzing bees collect my nectar sweet,
A symphony of life, where nature's bounty
meets.

The summer sun may scorch, the winter wind
may bite,
But through the seasons' cycle, I stand and take
the fight.
For resilience is my core, a spirit ever bold,
A testament to growth, in stories yet untold.

I may not be a rose, a symbol of grand cheer,
But in my simple beauty, life's message rings so
clear.
To bloom where planted, face the sun and rain,
And find your strength within, through sun and
storm and pain.

So let the wildflowers bloom, across the fields
so wide,
A tapestry of color, where spirits can't be tied.
For in our wildness lies a beauty to behold,
A story of resilience, waiting to unfold.

The Spring Tree

It's a time for a new beginning,
Which will be full of flowers and joy
It will be fresh and calm.

This is the time to restart,
Embracing a new life;
it will come upon and form.

You look up at the clear blue sky,
And make shapes of the clouds.
You laugh your unique laugh,
And wish you didn't need to go.

The perennials rebloom,
And the grass is up high.
You run through the meadow,
And enjoy the sight.

There are so many,
But this is one,
Leaves and branches are sprouting,
Filling the top with green.

There the colors which turn in fall,
And huge roots that can be seen.

Hopefully it won't get cut,
It's my friend,
And should be yours too.

You gape at the magnificent bark,
And are in awe of the luscious green.
You go lay underneath,
And I get an apple in between.

We pull out our favorite books,
Then we rest our backs,
Get in a comfortable position,
Or we drift off.

Melody

The melodic tune is calm
The instrumental vibration
As though everything
And more in its place
The rhythm goes through me
Filling my body with relaxation
Everything around me disappears
As I close my eyes slowly

The sound is as if there
Is the orchestra in my head
And a choral was made
The melodic tunes
One that puts someone to sleep,
A lullaby,
That did the same to me

When I wake up,
It comes back once more
I hum to it this time
Savoring every note.